How to Understand Your Financial Statement

The Key to Managing Your Business

WL Laney
AMERICAN HOPE SUCCESS

How to Understand Your Financial Statement

The Key to Managing Your Business

American Hope Success presents hope and success strategies for small to medium size businesses.
Copyright © 2017 by American Hope Success

WL Laney

All rights reserved. No part of this book may be reproduced in any manner whatsoever, and it may not be stored in a retrieval system, transmitted, or otherwise copied for public or private use without the written permission other than "fair use" of brief quotations embodied in articles and reviews.

ISBN-13: 978-1541025639

ISBN-10: 1541025636

Foreword

I have known WL Laney for several years and read all of his books. I admire his ability to cut through and capture the things that matter in business. In Seven Money Strategies, WL does it again.

As one of the founders of a software design and development company with offices in New York, USA, in Dublin, Ireland and in Bangalore, India, the biggest challenge I faced in building the business had less to do with motivating staff on three continents, or winning new business, or satisfying customers. It continues to be managing the money the company generates.

I am not for more government regulation of business, but there have been times I have wondered why there was not a common sense financial test every business founder must pass before registering a company. I certainly could have benefitted from it. Many entrepreneurs have little to no financial training and often do not understand their P&L statement or balance sheet. An idea typically motivates entrepreneurs to go out and do something about it. However, without understanding basic accounting, it is not too surprising to find yourself in a pickle sooner than expected.

I particularly like some of the lines in an Ernest Hemingway novel, The Sun Also Rises:

'How did you go bankrupt?' Bill asked." Two ways,' Mike said. 'Gradually and then suddenly.'

What I've found is that it is hard to stand back from a business and see things objectively when you are caught up in the daily pressures of running it. Having some means of detecting early warning signs is crucial. In a similar way to how you take care of your health, by getting a physical check-up annually, the same common sense principle applies to business: it is excellent advice to get regular check-ups for your business. In this book, WL provides you with the tools and guidance needed to do this effectively.

WL's suggestions to separate business and personal expenses, keep detailed and honest records, understand your books, manage growth and the most insightful of all, work on your business, not in your business, in my view represent sound business principles.

I encourage you to read WL's other business books, particularly "**Grow Your Business to Extreme Wealth.**" A curious thing about common sense is that it is not common at all. Rarer still is common sense based on experience and brought to life in a story. All of WL's books demonstrate it. There is plenty here to help businesspeople succeed more.

I hope you enjoy it as much as I have.

Noel Guinane Managing Director Blood & Treasure, Ltd.

Contents

How to Understand Your Financial Statement ... 2

The Key to Managing Your Business 2

Foreword 4

Introduction 12

Chapter 1 18

Chapter 2 28

Keep detailed records 28

Honest accounting 29

IRS suggestions/requirements 31

Records for gross receipts include: 32

Documents for purchases include: 33

Chapter 3 46

Scrutinize your financial statements 46

Annual financial checkup 48

Chapter 4 60

Focus on the bottom line 60

Financial Statements 62

   External users of financial information 66

Income Statement 68

Balance Sheet 77

Assets 78

Liabilities 83

Equity 86

Cash Flow Statement 90

Financial Analysis 98

Analytical Tools and Techniques - Ratios 100

Activity ratios 101

Total Asset Turnover 110

Liquidity Ratios 112

Solvency Ratios 118

Profitability Ratios 124

Gross Profit Margin 126

Operating Profit Margin 126

Pretax Margin 127

Net Profit Margin 128

Return on Assets - ROA............................ 128

Return on Equity 129

Horizontal Analysis 130

Break-even Analysis 138

   Sensitivity Analysis................................ *142*

Chapter 5 144

Manage your growth 144

Plan 149

Test your ideas 153

Attend seminars 154

Chapter 6 156

Chapter 7 164

Working on your Business 164

Understanding growth levels 169

   Existence *169*

   Survival *172*

   Success *177*

   Take-off *179*

   Maturity *180*

Introduction

The statistics vary depending on which survey you read, but the sad truth is that far too many start-up businesses fail. Some fold in the first year and others survive only three to five years; however, by the tenth year, some say up to 80 percent failed.

Almost everyone names money as a primary reason for failure; however, there are many other reasons for the high failure rate. Travis Thorpe, CEO, and founder of Boostability, names five top grounds for failure in an article for Inc. Magazine.

    1. Failure to market online

    2. Failure to listen to customers

    3. Failure to leverage future growth

4. Failure to adapt and grow when the market changes

5. Failure to track and measure marketing efforts

Todd Ballowe, a web developer for OnStrategy, gives ten common causes for business failure.

1. Failure to understand your market and customers

2. Opening a business in an industry that is not profitable

3. Failure to understand and communicate what you are selling

4. Inadequate financing

5. Reactive attitudes

6. Over-dependence on a single customer

7. No customer strategy

8. Not knowing when to say no

9. Poor management

10. No planning

All of these reasons are valid and worth your consideration. This book is about money. While we will look at some of the other reasons, my primary focus is on the secrets to success you can find hidden within your financial statement.

I believe you can avoid any of the reasons given for failure. You can operate a successful business if you pay attention to the details and get help in the areas where you are weak.

In my book **"How to Grow Your Business to Extreme Wealth,"** I wrote, the premise is business is a tool for developing your wealth, not just a means of escaping the drudgery of working for the other guy.

It is my sincere desire that you will read this book and discover the secrets hidden within your financial statement in time to save your business from failure. Or, you can use these principles to take your business to the next level of success.

Watch for these seven secrets to business success.

1. Keep your personal and business funds completely separate.
2. Maintain detailed financial records for your business.
3. Scrutinize your financial statements every month.
4. Focus your attention on the bottom line.
5. Manage your growth.
6. Manage your attitude toward money.
7. Work on, not in your business.

Chapter 1

Keep spending entirely separate, don't co-mingle personal and business expenses. This mistake made by many first-time entrepreneurs can have disastrous results. It is easy to look at the business account balance and feel rich because it has more money than a typical household account.

It is important to understand this is not your money yet. The balance looks good, but ongoing monthly expenses also encumber it.

Some years ago, I was operating a business with nearly 200 employees. When the salesman came into the office to pitch his product or service, it was easy to look at the bank account balance and say, "Sure, I've got enough money to cover that."

The problem was the account balance did not take into consideration expenses that were coming up and had to be paid.

For example, my monthly rent for 25 locations was close to $40,000. Fortunately, I spread the due dates throughout the month, but they all still needed to be accounted for before making unscheduled purchases.

I devised an Excel spreadsheet that allowed me to see what I needed to have set aside based on my daily cash flow to meet the rent and other needs before indiscriminately spending money just because there was a balance in the checkbook.

Accountant types may not have been impressed with my spreadsheet, but it certainly worked for me and allowed me a much better handle on controlling my expenditures before the money was "mine."

Rather than paying for personal expenses out of the company checkbook, I paid myself a salary and took a biweekly check like all the other employees.

For years, I joked that one of the joys of owning a business is getting paid last, if at all.

You should view this exactly for what it is: a sick joke.

If your business is not earning enough money to pay you, the owner, a livable wage, you need to question why you are working for free. If you designed your company as a nonprofit and you are independently wealthy, then I guess it's okay to pay yourself last if at all.

For illustration purposes, I'd like to tell you the first half of the Harriet story.

Some years ago, I started a business with an inexperienced financial partner. As good entrepreneurs, we calculated the cost of setting up the business and operating it until it could become profitable. We also each identified personal assets that we could liquidate if our calculation of time to profitability was off.

Harriet (not her real name) was my partner's wife. Her background as an interior decorator was both a help and a detriment as we were setting up the office.

Based on her desire for how the office should look, we spent too much on office furniture and decorations for what was supposed to be our franchise model, which we would sell to other aspiring entrepreneurs.

Don't get me wrong; I like nice things. I think it's valuable to have a successful looking office. But as a startup, we should have delayed some of those expenses until we could pay for them with profits rather than our startup cash.

The real shocker, though, came one morning when my financial backer partner announced that Harriet had spent the money, he committed to our start-up, to decorate and furnish their new home.

As you are aware, lack of capital is a primary reason that 80 percent of all startup companies fail in the first ten years. It is not necessarily poor planning as much as it is unanticipated stuff happening.

The challenge becomes how to keep the business afloat when the unexpected drains your capital or hinders your sales.

Many people fund their startups or keep their businesses afloat with personal credit cards. While it seems like an easy way to pay the bills, it can have some serious unintended consequences.

First, maxing out your personal credit cards can have a negative impact on your credit score. A poor credit score can make it nearly impossible to borrow money for equipment or to open a line of credit to balance the ups and downs of your cash flow.

A second and potentially more devastating result is that credit card debt can take you down personally if the business fails.

Entrepreneurs are risk-takers, by nature. This admirable quality may lead to fabulous results when the entrepreneur sees an opportunity, acts on it and starts a business that becomes wildly successful.

On the other hand, that same trait and determination to succeed regardless of

what happens can be the thing that takes the entrepreneur down.

I would like to say here –

If you go down,

please decide to get back up.

Starting a new business after a business  failure with credit that has been destroyed, assets that have been depleted and an ego that has been bruised is, at the least, very difficult.

Take it from me, though; you can make it. Do not let a single failure rob you of your financial future and destiny.

My congratulations for taking the time to read this book. There are methods you can use to detect the early warning signs of a financial weakness in the operation of your company.

Think of it like going to the doctor for an annual physical. That annual physical can detect the onset of a disease in a very early stage, and that early detection can make the cure much easier and more likely.

Do the same with your business. Get an annual checkup. Find out whether there are weaknesses in your financial statements. Later in this book, I will discuss financial ratios and how they can impact your business.

Take the time to learn how to evaluate your business compared to the industry standards using these financial ratios. They have been proven over time and can alert you to potential problems in your future.

Education, financial acumen, and early detection can keep your business from becoming one of the 80 percents.

Chapter 2

Keep detailed records

The shoebox accounting method may have worked in some bygone era, but believe me, it will not function for you today. The success of your business depends on complete, accurate financial statements.

You cannot operate your business in the financial dark. You must understand both revenue and expenses.

You must be able to comprehend economic principles and how they impact pricing your product and services, offering a fair salary to your employees and enjoying the profit you earn from the operation of your business.

Honest accounting

Do not yield to the temptation of keeping two sets of books. Stealing from Uncle Sam will have a more negative impact on you and your business than any potential savings in taxes paid out.

Consider your banker for a moment. How much confidence would your banker have in your second set of books when you apply for a loan of any size?

Think of the venture capital firm's response when you offer your second set of books while trying to raise money to grow your business to the next level.

Think of the prospective buyer for your business when you decide it's time to cash out and you offer a second set of books, and then try to convince the buyer of the profitability of your business.

I have worked with enough business buyers to recognize the red flags and the loss of confidence in everything else you say if you produce a second set of books.

You must pay your taxes. I don't enjoy taxes any more than the next person, but I do understand that if I try to cheat the system, I am saying that I am a dishonest person who cannot be trusted.

Since we are near the bottom of the tax rate (24.8%) list compared to other parts of the world, we probably should not complain.

IRS Suggestions/Requirements

The IRS requires accurate record keeping. According to the IRS, good records will help you:

- Monitor the progress of your business
- Prepare your financial statements
- Identify sources of your income
- Keep track of your deductible expenses
- Keep track of your basis in property
- Prepare your tax returns
- Support items reported on your tax returns

The following are some types of records you should keep:

- Gross receipts are the income you receive from your business. You should keep supporting documents that show the amounts and sources of your gross receipts.

Records for gross receipts include:

- Cash register tapes
- Deposit information (cash and credit sales)
- Receipt books - Invoices - Forms 1099 -MISC

Inventory purchases are the items you buy and resell to customers. If you are a manufacturer or producer, this includes the cost of all raw materials or parts purchased to manufacture your finished products. Your supporting documents should show the amount paid and that the amount was for purchases.

Documents for purchases include:

- Canceled checks or other materials that identify payee, amount, and proof of payment/electronic funds transferred
- Cash register tape receipts
- Credit card receipts and statements
- Invoices
- Expenses are the costs you incur (other than purchases) to carry on your business.

- Your supporting documents should show the amount paid, and a description that explains the amount was for a business expense.

Documents for expenses include:

- Canceled checks or other materials that identify payee, amount, and proof of payment/electronic funds transferred
- Cash register tapes
- Account statements
- Credit card receipts and statements
- Invoices
- Petty cash slips for small cash payments

- Expenses for travel, transportation, entertainment, and gifts must be tracked if you will claim deductions. You must be able to prove (substantiate) certain elements of expenses. For additional information, refer to IRS Publication 463, Travel, Entertainment, Gift, and Car Expenses.

Assets are the property, such as machinery and furniture, that you own and use in your business. You must keep records to verify certain information about your business assets. You need records to compute the annual depreciation, and to calculate the gain or loss when you sell the assets.

Documents for assets should show the following information:

- When and how you acquired the assets
- Purchase price o Cost of any improvements
- Section 179 deduction taken
- Deductions for depreciation
- Deductions taken for casualty losses, such as losses resulting from fires or storms o How you used the asset
- When and how you disposed of the asset
- Selling price
- Expenses of sale

The following documents may show this information.

- Purchase and sales invoices
- Real estate closing statements
- Canceled checks or other documents that identify payee, amount, and proof of payment/electronic funds transferred
- Employment taxes are specific records you must keep. Keep all records of employment for at least four years. For additional information, refer to Recordkeeping for Employers and IRS Publication 15, Circular E Employers Tax Guide.

The IRS suggests the following techniques for keeping records:

A good recordkeeping system includes a summary of your business transactions. Business operations are ordinarily summarized in books called journals and ledgers. You can buy them at your local stationery or office supply store.

A journal is a book in which you record each business transaction shown on your supporting documents. You may have to keep separate journals for transactions that occur frequently.

A ledger is a book that contains the totals from all of your journals. It is organized into different accounts.

Electronic records: All requirements that apply to hard copy books and files also apply to business records that are maintained using electronic accounting software, point-of-sale software, financial software or any other electronic documents system. The electronic system must provide a complete and accurate record of your data that is accessible to the IRS.

Whether you keep paper or electronic journals and ledgers depends on the type of business you are in. For example, a recordkeeping system for a small business might include:

- Business checkbook
- Daily and monthly summary of cash receipts
- Check disbursements journal

- Depreciation worksheet
- Employee compensation records

Note: The system you use to record business transactions will be more efficient if you follow good recordkeeping practices. For example, record expenses when they occur and identify the sources of income. It is best to record transactions daily. For additional information on how to record your business transactions, refer to IRS Publication 583, Starting a Business and Keeping Records.

According to the IRS, the length of time you should keep a document depends on the action, expense, or event the document records. You must keep your records that support an item of income, deduction or credit shown on your tax return until the period of limitations for that tax return runs out.

The period of limitations is the time in which you can amend your tax return to claim a credit or refund, or in which the IRS can assess additional fees.

The information below reflects the periods of limitations that apply to income tax returns. Unless otherwise stated, the years refer to the period after the return is filed. Returns filed before the due date are treated as filed on the due date.

> Note: Keep copies of your filed tax returns. They help in preparing future tax returns and making computations if you file an amended return.

Time limitations for income tax returns

1. Keep records for three years if situations (4), (5) and (6) below do not apply to you.
2. Maintain records for three years from the date you filed your original return, or two years from the date you paid the tax, whichever is later if you file a claim for credit or refund after you file your return.
3. Keep records for seven years if you file a claim for a loss from worthless securities or bad debt deduction.

4. Maintain records for six years if you do not report income that you should report, and it is more than 25% of the gross income shown on your return.
5. Keep records indefinitely if you do not file a return.
6. Maintain records forever if you submit a fraudulent return.
7. Keep employment tax records for at least four years after the date that the tax becomes due or is paid, whichever is later.

When deciding whether to keep a document or throw it away; first determine whether the records are connected to the property.

If so, the general guideline is to keep records relating to property until the period of limitations expires for the year in which you dispose of the property. You must keep these records to figure any depreciation, amortization, or depletion deduction and to figure the gain or loss when you sell or otherwise dispose of the property.

If you received property in a nontaxable exchange, your basis in that property is the same as the basis of the property you gave up, increased by any money you paid. You must keep the records on the old property, as well as on the new property until the period of limitations expires for the year in which you dispose of the new property.

Additionally, when your records are no longer needed for tax purposes, do not discard them until you check to see if you have to keep them longer for other uses. For example, your insurance company or creditors may require you to keep records longer than the IRS does.

Chapter 3

Scrutinize your financial statements

There is a science to reading a financial statement that many entrepreneurs do not understand. Think of your financial statement as a report card.

Not to be confused with keeping two sets of books, two very different kinds of financial statements are needed. The first is considered an external financial statement.

This type of financial statement is typically used for outsiders – bankers, investors, tax authorities or significant partners of the business. It is prepared based on **Generally Accepted Accounting Principles.**

The second, an internal financial statement typically for the business owner and management team is more flexible and may be more detailed with breakdowns by divisions or even product lines of the business. The internal report is usually done monthly for the sake of and convenience of day-to-day operating decisions made by management.

Some people believe in the viability of the company or their ability to pull it out of the abyss of loss and will give the company all they have. If the company ends in bankruptcy, these people will be there personally as well.

Other people see the handwriting on the wall and bail personally before they are forced to go down with the ship, so to speak.

An acquaintance confided that he had hidden thousands of dollars under the mattress before declaring bankruptcy for his company. He then used the cash to start recovering without the debt of the company.

My feeling on this is pretty black and white. If you are going take advantage of bankruptcy laws, you should follow the letter of the law and declare the all the assets as well as the liabilities.

Annual financial checkup

To protect and grow your business, schedule an annual checkup. This checkup would be in addition to tax visits with your accountant.

Jack's business was doing approximately 25 million dollars in annual revenue. Over time, his accounts receivable slipped into an average of 45 days for collection.

During an annual financial checkup, Jack and his accountant determined two things. One, they could realize approximately 1 million dollars in cash by shortening the collection time on receivables to 30 days. Two, they needed and devised a plan to make it a reality.

Of course, this brought on another problem  most any entrepreneur would welcome. How should they use an extra one million dollars for the business? Borrow less? Invest in new equipment? Hire staff to help grow the business?

Items to check annually

Some things to look out for are:

1. How will a lending institution view your company in its current financial condition?

2. What are the strengths and weaknesses of your operation?
3. What steps can you take that will likely improve your profitability?
4. What trends could signal problems in the near future?
5. How do your ratios and statistics compare to other similar-sized businesses in your industry?

A watchful eye is critical all year long, and not just for your annual financial checkup. I once had a trusted employee Walt, who worked a dual role. He was a senior manager, overseeing a group of managers who each had a team of four to ten members. His second role was watching the accounts payable, including the staff payroll.

One memorable day, Walt asked to talk with me in my office. "The bank will not honor our payroll checks this week." After picking myself up off the floor, I asked the obvious question, why?

It seemed that for three months, the bank had allowed us to overdraw our account every week for the amount of payroll. The branch manager of the bank received a call from corporate saying the unauthorized "loans" had to stop.

The bank did not want to lose a good customer, but drastic measures were in order.

At that time, I had three minor partners. We all had to go to the bank and sign for a loan. What a nightmare. I will never forget

 sitting in the new bank office – we were switched from the old branch, and the manager we had worked with was demoted. The manager of the new branch was laying out the rules, treating us as if we were a bunch of kids caught in a schoolyard fight. We sat and listened as he scolded us for not managing our money, and then he advised us of the terms of our new loan.

We would be required to submit a financial statement every month. We could not increase our salaries. The list went on and on.

With 200 employees waiting to get paid, we had no choice but to listen to this "blowhard" who knew nothing about the operation of our business exert his authority over our lives and our business.

When it was over, we all signed for the company's note, the money was deposited into our account, the employees were paid on time, and we went on our merry way.

There are two points to this story. First, you simply have to stay on top of the finances of your company. If we had not been such a good customer, the bank might not have given us the loan to satisfy the needs of our immediate payroll. You could imagine the damage to the company if we were unable to meet payroll.

Our competitors would have had a heyday when our employees took their story with them while looking for new employment.

Second, an early indication of pending trouble would have given me an opportunity to solve the issue before it became a "this has to be fixed today" problem.

I got the last laugh, though, and it was one of the greatest moments in my business career.

When the dust settled, I sold an asset and had enough money to pay off the loan at the bank and buy out my partners. After the scolding at the bank, they were more than happy to sell.

The fun moment was when I went to the bank and asked to speak with the manager. I told him we were not going to be able to make our first payment on the new loan. The look on his face was priceless.

Then I informed him I was paying it off entirely. My only regret was not making him squirm longer. Yes, I know that the man with the money gets to make the rules.

As an independent business owner, I wanted a little more respect. The banker was well aware that my trusted employee was the fly in the ointment.

Never let anyone put you in that position.

Read and understand your financial statements.

Check the numbers to make sure nothing is being hidden. Be proactive in managing your finances. Do not become a business failure by neglecting your cash flow and profitability. If you don't understand your financial statements, get the help of a professional who does!

Don't be the culprit.

That takes care of the employee. What about you?

I will call this guy Sad Sam. Sam owned a great company with multiple locations, strong cash flow, and a great industry. In fact, Sam had so much going for him; he was asked to participate in a roll-up in his industry.

The developer chose Sam because of his experience working at a top management level in a public company in the same industry. Sam's private company demonstrated his ability to manage and resulted in the offer to be president of the new "roll-up" company whose goal was a public offering.

After months of working on the roll-up with some really amazing results, it all came crashing down on Sad Sam. Sam was caught with his hands in the cookie jar.

Sam's company was a staffing company. He placed temporary workers in the field for client companies. Sam paid the temps' wages, employment taxes, the employers' half of social security, and worker's comp, and he withheld taxes for the employee.

As you can imagine, this was a significant amount of money every week. Sam was good with people as evidenced by his success in his previous position with the publicly traded staffing company. He knew the industry extremely well and seemed the perfect person for the new roll-up.

What did not show initially was his lack of understanding the importance of financial management of a small business. Sam succumbed to the temptation that sucks in many other entrepreneurs.

He wrote the check to the IRS and the state for taxes and withholdings. Then he stuck it in the drawer instead of putting it in the mail.

When it came time for the audit, his lack of financial acumen became a glaring truth for all to see.

Sam lost a golden opportunity to be president and part owner of a highly successful public staffing company. Worse yet, he lost his business to the IRS for lack of payment.

The IRS takes a very dim view of business owners spending their employees' money on anything but the trust fund for the employees' taxes.

Chapter 4

Focus on the bottom line

Common sense seems to agree that the focus of business has to be on the bottom line. If you are losing 10 cents on every dollar of sales, increasing sales is not necessarily the answer to profitability.

Recently I was asked if I could assist in setting up a nonprofit organization. My smart alec reply was simple. Set up a regular business and then spend more than you earn. Voilà: a nonprofit organization.

In a recent Forbes Magazine article, Matthew Garret hit the nail on the head: "Look at the Triple Bottom Line." Examine three areas carefully – 1) net income from operations, 2) net equity and 3) net cash from operations.

Any list of reasons for business failure includes money. The natural assumption is that the entrepreneur did not have enough money to get the business successfully off the ground.

My experience shouts, No. That is an oversimplification. It's more likely mismanagement of the money on hand.

Let's look at financial ratios to see how to manage the money and cash flow of your business better.

Financial Statements

Understanding your financial statement is crucial to the success of any company. Presenting financial statements according to applied standards of one country is a legal requirement for every business. Whether financial statements are presented according to International Financial Reporting Standards (IFRS – adapted by most of the countries), or Generally Accepted Accounting Principles (GAAP – used in the US and some other countries), the content and the presentation form of financial statements may change.

Financial statements scan the company and present financial results from different dimensions to different users that use the information to take decisions for the future of the enterprise. Users of the information presented in financial statements can be classified into two groups: internal users and external users.

Internal users of financial information

- **Management**: business managers use the information to analyze company's performance and the current position to make decisions and ensure the company is on the right track and improve future results.

- **Employees**: their financial well-being is highly depended on the performance of the company where they work (job security, benefits, profit-sharing plans, collective agreements, etc.), so financial statements can provide valuable information for them.
  - **Owners:** they need the information to determine whether the business is profitable or not, to take courses of action with their investment based on that information. Note that in small businesses, owners usually manage the company, while for large enterprises, owners often

(shareholders or stockholders) trust the management to manage their business in their best interest through agency relationship contracts.

External users of financial information

Government: they are interested in the financial performance of the company for tax and regulatory purposes.

Lenders: they need the financial information to assess the creditworthiness of the business, whether it can repay the loan and interest.

Suppliers: similar to creditors, they are interested to know whether the company can pay its trade obligations when they are due.

Investors: different investors depending on the size of the enterprise, angel investors, venture capitalists, or for public companies, institutional and retail investors in stock market need financial information presented in financial statements to take d their decisions on their investment.

Customers: they need the information to assess financial stability of their suppliers, especially in the case of long-term contracts. Note that clients may include not only consumers, but also other firms that purchase inventory, services, and supplies.

General public: researchers, analysts, media, students, etc. may be interested in financial information for specific reasons.

There are three basic financial statements:

- **Income Statement**
- **Balance Sheet.**
- **Cash Flow Statements**

Income Statement

Usually, the process of building financial statements starts with the income statement, as the information presented in the income statement is an essential element for balance sheet (net income in retained earnings). The income statement shows financial results of a company from its business activity over a period of time, showing revenues the company generated over that period and expenses it incurred. The income statement is also referred to as "profit and loss statement," "statement of earnings," or "statement of operations." The income statement basic equation is:

Revenues – Expenses = Net Income (Net loss)

Revenues refer to the amount of money that company generates from the sale of its goods and services during the reporting period that income statement covers. Companies often report revenues as **net income** which means revenues adjusted for allowances and estimated returns. Revenues represent inflows in the business, and they increase the final result of business activities – net income.

Expenses refer to the amounts that business incurs in its operations of generating revenues, including here, the cost of goods sold, operating expenses, incurrences of liabilities (interest), and taxes. Expenses represent outflows, and they decrease the net income.

The income statement includes gains and losses that may result from the primary business activity or other events and may increase or decrease economic benefits. For example, a company may sell its unused equipment or part of land that is no longer needed. The difference between the net price and the book value is reported as gain (if the sale price is higher than the book value), or loss (if the sale price is lower than the book value). If the company has a controlling interest in a subsidiary, it has to report its share of net income in the subsidiary as noncontrolling interest, or minority (owners') interest.

Figure 1: Income Statement

XYZ Company - Income Statement	31-Dec-15	31-Dec-14	31-Dec-13
Net revenues	$770,889.00	$871,104.57	$686,091.21
Cost of good sales (COGS)	$412,650.00	$478,674.00	$383,764.50
Gross Profit	**$358,239.00**	**$392,430.57**	**$302,326.71**
Selling, general and administrative expenses	$135,700.00	$132,986.00	$104,489.00
Depreciation expenses	$70,000.00	$70,000.00	$65,000.00
Operating profit (EBIT - Earning Before Interest and Taxes)	**$152,539.00**	**$189,444.57**	**$132,837.71**
Internet expense	$9,200.00	$12,480.00	$10,100.00
Income before tax	**$143,339.00**	**$176,964.57**	**$122,737.71**
Tax	$31,534.00	$38,932.00	$27,002.00
Income from continuing operations	**$111,805.00**	**$138,032.57**	**$95,735.71**
Earning (losses) from discontinues operations, net of tax	$2,304.00	$4,400.00	$3,300.00
Net income	**$109,501.00**	**$133,632.57**	**$99,035.71**

Gross profit is the amount that remains after subtracting the direct cost incurred in producing the product or delivering the

71

service from net revenues. These costs may include expenses for raw materials, wage expenses for employees involved in the production process, etc. **Operating profit** known as **EBIT** (earnings before interest and taxes) is the amount that remains after subtracting operating expenses necessary for the business activity of a company, before deducting interest expense. Operating expenses may include selling, general, administrative, research and development, depreciation and other expenses. **Income before tax** is the amount that remains after subtracting interest expense from operating profit. When adding depreciation and amortization amounts to operating profit the result is **EBITDA** (earnings before interest, taxes, depreciation and amortization), which is the purest measure of company's operating performance before the impact of financial decisions, accounting decisions (since depreciation and amortization are not material expenses), and taxes. **Income before taxes** is calculated after interest expense is deducted from operating profit. Finally, after the deduction of taxes from the income before taxes (taxes are calculated as the tax rate * income before taxes), and the addition of net gains or losses, the result is **net income,** referred to as the "bottom line." Net income can be defined in different ways, and the definition may lead to changing the way the income statement is structured. The general definition of net income known as the basic equation of income statement is presented above, as net income is equal to revenues minus expenses. Another way how net income can be defined is as revenues plus other income plus gains minus expenses. And another way equals net income with income from the business activities minus expenses from business activities, plus other income minus other expenses, plus gains minus losses.

The figure below is Nike Inc. comprehensive statements of income presented in millions of USD. From this document can be seen the increasing trends in revenue and net income, and can be proceeded with calculating margins (both trends and margins will be discussed later), and further financial analysis. The information presented here can be used for in-depth analysis from internal and external financial analysis and can be critical in decision-making processes by many users of this financial information. This income statement along with other financial statements is filed by Nike to U.S. Securities and Exchange Commission.

Figure 2: Nike Consolidated Statements of Income ($ in millions)

Consolidated Statements Of Income - USD ($) $ in Millions	12 Months Ended		
	May 31, 2016	May 31, 2015	May 31, 2014
Income Statement [Abstract]			
Revenues	$ 32,376	$ 30,601	$ 27,799
Cost of sales	17,405	16,534	15,353
Gross profit	14,971	14,067	12,446
Demand creation expense	3,278	3,213	3,031
Operating overhead expense	7,191	6,679	5,735
Total selling and administrative expense	10,469	9,892	8,766
Interest expense (income), net	19	28	33
Other (income) expense, net	(140)	(58)	103
Income before income taxes	4,623	4,205	3,544
Income tax expense	863	932	851
NET INCOME	$ 3,760	$ 3,273	$ 2,693
Earnings per common share:			
Basic (in dollars per share)	$ 2.21	$ 1.90	$ 1.52
Diluted (in dollars per share)	2.16	1.85	1.49
Dividends declared per common share (in dollars per share)	$ 0.62	$ 0.54	$ 0.47

Source: www.sec.gov

Balance Sheet

The balance sheet presents a company's financial position at a point in time. It is a snapshot of company's resources (assets) and its sources of capital (where assets come from – owners' equity and liabilities/debt). It is also known as the statement of financial position or statement of financial condition. The balance sheet basic equation is:

Assets = Liabilities + Equity

Assets are resources that a company owns and controls as results of past activities and expects to generate future economic benefits from their use.

Liabilities are what a company owes. They are obligations arising from past activities, which will require outflows from the company to settle them.

Equity is owners' claim on company's assets after deducting the liabilities. It is also known as owners' equity, shareholders' equity, or stockholders' equity. Equity is what remains from assets after deducting liabilities.

Assets

Current Assets

7As can be seen from the balance sheet below, the ordering of balance sheet lines is done in order of their liquidity, i.e. how fast can every line be turned into cash, as cash represents the perfect liquid asset.

Cash and cash equivalents include cash and its equivalents, which are short-term highly liquid investment assets, such as, Treasury bills, commercial bills, and money market funds.

Marketable securities include financial assets that are traded in the public market, such as, equity securities, Treasury bills, bonds, and notes.

Accounts receivable are assets that represent amounts that customers (other firms or final consumers) owe to the company for goods and/or services sold on credit.

Inventories are physical goods for sale that company is currently holding and expects to sell either as finished products or as inputs (raw materials and work-in-process goods).

Other assets include current assets, not material to be shown separately. Thus they are grouped together in one line, such as prepaid expenses and deferred tax assets.

Figure 3: XYZ Balance Sheet

XYZ Company - Balance Sheet	31-Dec-15	31-Dec-14	31-Dec-13
Cash and its equivalents	$157,851.64	$165,744.22	$149,959.06
Marketable securities	$92,533.72	$97,160.41	$87,907.03
Accounts receivable	$70,761.08	$74,299.13	$67,223.03
Inventories	$179,624.28	$188,605.49	$170,643.07
Other current assets	$43,545.28	$45,722.54	$41,368.02
Total current assets	**$544,316.00**	**$ 571,531.80**	**$ 517,100.20**
Propoerty, plant, and equipment	$305,480.76	$320,754.80	$290,206.72
Investment property	$162,923.07	$171,069.23	$154,776.92
Intangible assets	$142,557.69	$149,685.57	$135,429.80
Financial assets	$172,322.48	$180,938.60	$163,706.36
Total non-current assets	**$783,284.00**	**$822,448.20**	**$744,119.80**
Total assets	**$1,327,600.00**	**$1,393,980.00**	**$1,261,220.00**
Accounts payable	$94,843.74	$99,585.93	$90,101.56
Notes payable and current portion of long term debt	$82,364.30	$86,482.52	$78,246.09
Accrues liabilities	$52,413.65	$55,034.33	$49,792.97
Unearned revenue	$19,967.10	$20,965.46	$18,968.75
Total current liabilites	**$249,588.80**	**$262,068.24**	**$237,109.36**
Long-term financial liabilities	$306,994.22	$322,343.94	$291,644.51
Deferred tax-liabilities	$67,388.98	$70,758.42	$64,019.53
Total non-current liabilities	**$374,383.20**	**$393,102.36**	**$355,664.04**
Total liabilities	**$623,972.00**	**$655,170.60**	**$592,773.40**
Contributed capital by owners (issued capital or common stock)	$232,197.24	$243,807.10	$220,587.38
Preferred shares	$56,290.24	$59,104.75	$53,475.73
Treasury stock	$35,885.03	$37,679.28	$34,090.78
Retained earnings	$309,596.32	$325,076.14	$294,116.50
Accumulated other comprehensive income	$48,550.33	$50,977.85	$46,122.82
Noncontrolling interest (minority interest)	$21,108.84	$22,164.28	$20,053.40
Total equity	**$703,628.00**	**$738,809.40**	**$668,446.60**

Non-current assets

Non-current assets include assets that the company uses in its operation activities for longer than a year.

81

Property, plant, and equipment (PPE) include tangible assets that are used in operations for longer periods than one year, such as, land, buildings, machinery, furniture, natural resources, etc.

Investment property includes (real estate) properties that are not used in the production of goods or services or for administrative purposes but are purchased to earn rental income or capital appreciation.

Intangible assets are identifiable non-monetary assets without physical substance, such as patents, licenses, trademarks, goodwill, etc.

Financial assets include financial instruments that at the moment of creation give an asset to one entity and a liability to another. They include investment in securities issued by another company, financial derivatives, etc.

Liabilities

Current liabilities

Current liabilities are obligation that the company expects to settle within one year of its operating cycle

Accounts payable include amounts the firm owes to other firms (suppliers) for goods and services purchased on credit.

Notes payable and current portion of long-term debt are liabilities that the company owns to creditors for the debt it borrowed from them. Current portion of long-term debt (liabilities) is the amount that has to be paid within one operating year from the long-term debt.

Accrued liabilities include expenses that have to be recorded but have a due date of payment (settlement) further in the future, beyond the operating year.

Unearned revenue is a liability that results when the company collects the cash without delivering goods or providing service.

Non-current liabilities

Long-term financial liabilities include liabilities with long-term maturity, such as bank loans, notes payable, bonds payable, etc.

Deferred tax liabilities come as a result of timing differences between the company's income as reported in financial statements and company's income reported for tax purposes

Equity

Capital contributed by owners is the amount contributed to the company by owners represented as common stock or issued capital.

Preferred shares, also known as preferred stock sometimes is classified as a liability as it displays liability characteristics since it gets paid dividends at a specific rate and it is prioritized higher than common stock in the claiming hierarchy. Unlike common stock, preferred stock does not grant voting rights to its holder.

Treasury stock is equity that has been reacquired by the company from its previous holders but has not been retired yet.

Retained earnings are the undistributed earnings of the company since its beginning of operations that have been reinvested in the company.

Accumulated other comprehensive income include all changes in the equity such as issuing stock, reacquiring stock, and paying dividends.

Non-controlling interest (minority interest) is shareholders' shares in a subsidiary, which is not wholly owned by the company.

The figure below shows the balance sheet of Nike that can be used for different-purpose financial analysis by internal and external users of the information presented in this balance sheet.

Consolidated Balance Sheets - USD ($) $ in Millions	May 31, 2016	May 31, 2015
Current assets:		
Cash and equivalents	$ 3,138	$ 3,852
Short-term investments	2,319	2,072
Accounts receivable, net	3,241	3,358
Inventories	4,838	4,337
Prepaid expenses and other current assets	1,489	1,968
Total current assets	15,025	15,587
Property, plant and equipment, net	3,520	3,011
Identifiable intangible assets, net	281	281
Goodwill	131	131
Deferred income taxes and other assets	2,439	2,587
TOTAL ASSETS	21,396	21,597
Current liabilities:		
Current portion of long-term debt	44	107
Notes payable	1	74
Accounts payable	2,191	2,131
Accrued liabilities	3,037	3,949
Income taxes payable	85	71
Total current liabilities	5,358	6,332
Long-term debt	2,010	1,079
Deferred income taxes and other liabilities	1,770	1,479
Commitments and contingencies		
Redeemable preferred stock	0	0
Shareholders' equity:		
Capital in excess of stated value	7,786	6,773
Accumulated other comprehensive income	318	1,246
Retained earnings	4,151	4,685
Total shareholders' equity	12,258	12,707
TOTAL LIABILITIES AND SHAREHOLDERS' EQUITY	21,396	21,597
Class A Convertible Common Stock Shareholders' equity:		
Common stock	0	0
Class B Common Stock Shareholders' equity:		
Common stock	$ 3	$ 3

Figure 4: Nike Balance Sheet

Source: www.sec.gov

Cash Flow Statement

The cash flow statement provides information on the cash payments and received by the company for a period of time. While the income statement is built on the accrual basis, the cash flow statement is based on the cash method and displays comprehensive information on the cash generated and spent, not only in operating activities but financing and investing as well.

There are two methods of presenting the cash flow statement: direct and indirect method.

The direct method shows each line converted to cash. The main advantage of this approach is that it clearly presents operating cash coming and going from the company in detail. Therefore, it provides more information than the indirect method.

The indirect method converts net income to operating cash flow by adjusting cash transactions that affect net income. This method is useful to understand the differences between net income and operating cash flow.

The change in cash is a result of company's operating, investing, and financing activities:

      Operating cash flow

+   Investing cash flow

+   Financing cash flow

= Change in cash balance

+ Beginning cash balance

= Ending cash balance

Cash flow from operating activities (CFO) represents inflows and outflows of cash resulting from company's operating activities, which effect company's net income.

Cash flow from financing activities (CFF) represents inflows and outflows of cash resulting from obtaining and disposing company's capital.

Cash flow from investing activities (CFI) represents inflows and outflows of cash resulting from acquiring and selling long-term assets and other investments.

Figure 5: Cash Flow Statement

XYZ Company - Cash Flow Statement	31-Dec-15	31-Dec-14	31-Dec-13
Net profit	$109,501.00	$133,632.57	$99,035.71
Gain from sale of machinery	$19,000.00	$8,800.00	$3,300.00
Depretiation	$70,000.00	$70,000.00	$65,000.00
Subtotal	$198,501.00	$194,832.57	$167,335.71
Increase in accounts receivable	$3,538.05	$7,076.11	$2,900.00
Increase in inventories	$8,981.21	$17,962.43	$4,323.00
Decrease in prepaid expenses	$1,741.81	$3,483.62	$2,988.00
Increase in accounts payable	$4,742.19	$9,484.37	$3,111.00
Increase in accrued liabilities	$2,620.68	$5,241.36	$1,090.00
Operating cash flow (CFO)	**$176,877.05**	**$238,080.47**	**$181,747.71**
Cash from sale of machinery	$31,130.00	$9,900.00	$12,000.00
Purchase of plant and equipment	$39,800.00	$44,000.00	$17,880.00
Cash flow from investment (CFI)	$8,670.00	$34,100.00	$5,880.00
Sale of bonds	$11,500.00	$13,000.00	$0.00
Repurchase of stock	$0.00	$4,000.00	$13,000.00
Cash dividends	$2,200.00	$3,300.00	$900.00
Cash flow from financing	**$9,300.00**	**$5,700.00**	**$13,900.00**
Cash flow from operations	$176,877.05	$238,080.47	$181,747.71
Cash flow from investments	$8,670.00	$34,100.00	$5,880.00
Cash flow from financing	$9,300.00	$5,700.00	$13,900.00
Total cash flow	$177,507.05	$209,680.47	$161,967.71

As can be seen from the figure above, cash inflows and outflows are grouped into operating, investing and financing categories that when added together show the total cash flow during the reporting period. The figure below shows cash flow classifications according to US GAAP.

Figure 7: Cash Flow Classifications according to US GAAP

Operating Activities	
Inflows	Outflows
Cash from sales	Cash paid for salaries, accounts payables and other sort-term settlements
Divident, interest and other payments received	Cash paid for other expenses
Sale proceeds from securities	Cash paid to purchase trading securities
	Interest paid
	Taxes paid

Investing Activities	
Inflows	Outflows
Sale proceeds from the sale of fixed assets	Cash paid to purchase fixed assets
Sale proceeds from equity and debt investments	Cash paid to purchase equity and debt investments
Principal received from the loan lent to others	Loans loaned to others

Financing Activities	
Inflows	Outflows
Principal of the issued debt	Principal paid on the borrowed debt
Proceeds from issuing shares	Cash paid for reacquiring stock
	Dividends paid to shareholders

To continue with the Nike example below is presented Nike consolidated statement of cash flows. From this statement users of this financial information can analyze how Nike manages its cash and creditors may gain useful information about Nike's liquidity.

Figure 8: Nike consolidated cash flow statement

Consolidated Statements of Cash Flows - USD ($) $ in Millions	12 Months Ended		
	May 31, 2016	May 31, 2015	May 31, 2014
Cash provided by operations:			
Net income	$ 3,760	$ 3,273	$ 2,693
Income charges (credits) not affecting cash:			
Depreciation	649	606	518
Deferred income taxes	(80)	(113)	(11)
Stock-based compensation	236	191	177
Amortization and other	13	43	68
Net foreign currency adjustments	98	424	56
Changes in certain working capital components and other assets and liabilities:			
Decrease (increase) in accounts receivable	60	(216)	(298)
(Increase) in inventories	(590)	(621)	(505)
(Increase) in prepaid expenses and other current assets	(161)	(144)	(210)
(Decrease) increase in accounts payable, accrued liabilities and income taxes payable	(889)	1,237	525
Cash provided by operations	3,096	4,680	3,013
Cash used by investing activities:			
Purchases of short-term investments	(5,367)	(4,936)	(5,386)
Maturities of short-term investments	2,924	3,655	3,932
Sales of short-term investments	2,386	2,216	1,126
Investments in reverse repurchase agreements	150	(150)	0
Additions to property, plant and equipment	(1,143)	(963)	(880)
Disposals of property, plant and equipment	10	3	3
Decrease (increase) in other assets, net of other liabilities	6	0	(2)
Cash used by investing activities	(1,034)	(175)	(1,207)
Cash used by financing activities:			
Net proceeds from long-term debt issuance	981	0	0
Long-term debt payments, including current portion	(106)	(7)	(60)
(Decrease) increase in notes payable	(67)	(63)	75
Payments on capital lease obligations	(7)	(19)	(17)
Proceeds from exercise of stock options and other stock issuances	507	514	383
Excess tax benefits from share-based payment arrangements	281	218	132
Repurchase of common stock	(3,238)	(2,534)	(2,628)
Dividends — common and preferred	(1,022)	(899)	(799)
Cash used by financing activities	(2,671)	(2,790)	(2,914)
Effect of exchange rate changes on cash and equivalents	(105)	(83)	(9)
Net (decrease) increase in cash and equivalents	(714)	1,632	(1,117)
Cash and equivalents, beginning of year	3,852	2,220	3,337
CASH AND EQUIVALENTS, END OF YEAR	3,138	3,852	2,220
Cash paid during the year for:			
Interest, net of capitalized interest	70	53	53
Income taxes	748	1,262	856
Non-cash additions to property, plant and equipment	252	206	167
Dividends declared and not paid	$ 271	$ 240	$ 209

Source: www.sec.gov

Financial Analysis

Financial analysis is a process that encompasses a cycle of six steps:

1. **Define the purpose of analysis.**

    What is the nature of the analysis?

Valuation equity, credit application analysis, issuing new stock or debt, etc.

2. **Collect input data.** Sources may include financial statements, other financial data, industry report, discussions with management, market analysis, etc.

3. **Process data.** The outputs of this stage include adjusted financial statements, forecasts, ratios graphs, etc.

4. **Analyze and interpret the processed data.**

5. **Develop and communicate conclusions and recommendations.**
6. **Follow up.**

In this chapter, we will focus on analytical tools and interpreting the processes data.

Analytical Tools and Techniques - Ratios

Financial ratios used in financial analysis can be grouped in five categories:

- **Activity ratios**

- **Liquidity ratios**

- **Solvency ratios**

- **Profitability ratios**

For the purpose of our analysis we will use 2014 data from the income statement presented on page 72, and the balance sheet presented on page 77.

Activity ratios

Activity ratios measure the efficiency of a company in managing its assets to generate revenue. The data used in activity ratios is usually a combination from both, income statement and balance sheet. The most commonly used activity ratios include:

- **Inventory turnover**
- **Days of inventory turnover (DOH)**
- **Receivables turnover**
- **Days of sales outstanding (DSO)**
- **Payables turnover**
- **Number of days of payables**
- **Working capital turnover**
- **Fixed asset turnover**
- **Total asset turnover**

Inventory Turnover and Days of Inventory on Hand (DOH)

This ratio shows how fast the company turns inventory into cash. Companies usually try to have a higher inventory turnover as that that is an indicator of a higher effectiveness.

$$Inventory\ turnover = \frac{Cost\ of\ good\ sold\ (COGS)}{Average\ inventory} = \frac{478{,}674}{179{,}624} = 2.66$$

$$Average\ Inventory\ [1] = \frac{Inventory\ in\ 2014 + inventory\ from\ 2013}{2}$$

---

[1] Same calculation is applied for average receivables, average payables, average WC, average fixed assets, and average assets.

$$DOH = \frac{Number\ of\ days\ in\ period}{Inventory\ Turnover} = \frac{360}{2.66} = 135.34$$

As can be seen from the calculations above, this company, in average buys inventory and sells it 2.66 times per year, and it takes 135 days to sell the inventory from the moment it purchases it. These numbers may be big or small, depending on the industry this company operates in. If the company sells durable goods, inventory turnover is expected to be smaller and DOH number bigger than for non-durable goods.

Receivables Turnover and Days of Sales Outstanding (DSO)

DSO represents the time it takes for a company to collect the cash from its sales (on credit) and Receivables Turnover Ratio shows how many times a year a company collects its cash from sales.

$$Receivables\ turnover = \frac{Revenues}{Average\ Receivables} = \frac{871,104}{70,761} = 12.31$$

$$DSO = \frac{Number\ of\ days\ in\ period}{Receivables\ turnover} = \frac{360}{12.31} = 29.24$$

A high number on receivables turnover (and a low number in DSO, respectively) suggests that company is efficient in collecting its cash. If the number is too high, however, it could mean that the company is not flexible and could lose potential sales. A low number means company might not be efficient in its collection and credit procedures.

Payables Turnover and the Number of Days of Payables

Payables turnover ratio refers to the number of times the company pays off its suppliers within the reported period, and the Number of Days of Payables shows the number of days it takes for the company to pay its suppliers.

$$\textit{Payables Turnover} = \frac{\textit{Total Purchases}}{\textit{Average Accounts Payable}} =$$

$$\frac{496{,}636}{94{,}844} = 5.24$$

Total purchases = Ending inv. (2014) + COGS (2014) – Beginning Inv. (2013)

Number of Days of Payables =

$$\frac{\textit{Number of days in period}}{\textit{Payables Turnover}} = \frac{360}{5.24} = 68.75$$

A high number of payables turnover relative to the industry (and small Number of Days of Payables) could indicate that the company is not utilizing credit enough; a low number could mean the company is facing troubles on paying its obligations to suppliers.

Working Capital Turnover

Working capital represents the difference between current assets and current liabilities. Working capital turnover shows how efficiently the company utilizes its working capital to generate revenues.

$$Working\ Capital\ Turnover = \frac{Revenue}{Average\ working\ capital} = \frac{871,104}{294,727} = 2.96$$

A higher Working Capital Turnover shows efficiency for a company, and vice-versa.

Fixed Asset Turnover

This ratio measures the efficiency of a company in generating revenues from its investment in fixed assets.

$$Fixed\ Asset\ Turnover = \frac{Revenue}{Average\ Net\ Fixed\ Assets} = \frac{871,105}{305481} = 2.85$$

A high Fixed Asset Turnover ratio relative to the industry indicates that the company is efficient in utilizing its assets, while a low number indicates inefficiency, capital-intensive industry, or that the business is not operating at full capacity.

Total Asset Turnover

This ratio measures the efficiency of a company to generate revenue from its total assets. It is helpful to analyze this ratio against Working Capital Turnover and Fixed Asset Turnover as it can help to find inefficiencies in different groups of assets.

$$Total\ Asset\ Turnover = \frac{Revenue}{Average\ Total\ Assets} = \frac{871,105}{1,393,980} = 0.62$$

This number means that for every dollar of this company's assets, it generates 0.62 dollars in sales. This ratio reflects strategic choices of management between labor-intensive and capital-intensive approaches.

111

Liquidity Ratios

Liquidity ratios show a company's ability to pay for its short-term liabilities. The most commonly used liquidity ratios include:

- **Current Ratio**

- **Quick Ratio**

- **Cash Ratio**

- **Defensive Interval Ratio**

- **Cash Conversion Cycle (Net Operating Cycle)**

Current Ratio, Quick Ratio, and Cash Ratio

Current ratio shows company's ability to pay short-term liabilities with current assets. Basically, it shows how much debt (expected to mature in a short-term period) can the company pay with cash and other (current) assets expected to be turned into cash within a short-term period.

The quick ratio is more conservative than current ratio as it calculates company's liquidity by excluding less liquid current assets such as inventory and other assets, such as, prepaid expenses that may not be turned into cash anymore.

The most conservative liquidity ratio is the cash ratio and it is usually used in a crisis situation. When calculating the cash ratio of one company, only cash and highly marketable securities are used.

$$Current\ Ratio = \frac{Current\ assets}{Current\ liabilities} = \frac{571{,}532}{262{,}068} = 2.18$$

$$Quick\ Ratio = \frac{Current\ assets - inventories - other\ assets}{Current\ liabilities} = \frac{337{,}204}{262{,}068} = 1.29$$

Cash Ratio =

$$\frac{C.assets - inventories - other\ assets - accounts\ receivable}{Current\ liabilities} = \frac{262{,}905}{262{,}068} = 1$$

As can be seen from the example on the previous page, for every dollar of current liabilities, company owns 2.18 dollars of current assets, and this company results to be liquid even according to quick ratio and cash ratio. When the company is illiquid, its chances to take on additional borrowing decrease.

Defensive Interval Ratio

This ratio measures how long can the company pay its expenses from its current liabilities without receiving any additional money. In many cases, this is considered more useful than other liquidity ratios, as it measures company's liquidity against its expenses rather than liabilities.

$$\text{Defensive Cash Ratio} = \frac{\text{Current assets}}{\text{Daily operating expenses}} = \frac{571{,}531}{369} = 1{,}547$$

Daily operating expenses =

$$\frac{\text{Annual operating expenses} - \text{noncash charges}}{360} =$$

$$\text{Daily operating expenses} = \frac{202{,}986 - 70{,}000}{360} = 369$$

Noncash charges = Amortization + Depreciation + Depletion

Noncash charges = 70,000

This ratio shows that the company would be able to pay its expenses for 1,547 days without receiving any additional money, only from cash and sale of its other current assets. It is called defensive interval ratio because it uses company's current assets, which are known as defensive assets.

Cash Conversion Cycle (Net Operating Cycle)

This ratio shows how long it takes from the moment when the company invests in working capital until it collects the cash.

Cash Conversion Cycle = DOH + DSO + Nr. of Days of Payables = 95.8

As we can see, it takes around 96 days for the company to receive the cash from sales from the moment it invests its money.

Solvency Ratios

Solvency ratios measure a company's ability to meet its long-term liabilities. Solvency focuses on the amount of debt a company owes, and gives information on the level of earnings and cash flow that it needs to generate in order to pay for it. The most common solvency ratios include:

- **Debt-to-Assets Ratio**

- **Debt-to-Equity Ratio**

- **Financial Leverage Ratio**

- **Interest Coverage Ratio**

Debt-to-Assets-Ratio

This ratio measures the percentage of total assets financed with debt. A high ratio for a company means weaker solvency and more financial risk. However, it is worth noted that debt has a lower cost than equity, due to shareholders being residual claimants in company's assets.

$$Debt\text{-}to\text{-}Assets\ Ratio = \frac{Total\ liabilities}{Total\ assets} = \frac{655{,}171}{1{,}393{,}980} = 0.47$$

From the calculations above, it results that 47% of company's assets are financed with debt, or from every dollar of assets, 0.47 dollars come from debt. This number typically does not present a risky scenario for this company.

Debt-to-Equity Ratio

This ratio weights debt and equity against each other. If the result is 1.0, it means that company's assets are equally financed with debt and equity. It is worth noted that, in many cases, companies use the market value of equity, rather than its book value.

$$Debt\text{-}to\text{-}Equity\ Ratio = \frac{Total\ liabilities}{Total\ equity} = \frac{655{,}171}{738{,}809} = 0.89$$

As can be seen, for every dollar of equity, the company has 0.89 dollars of debt.

Financial Leverage Ratio

This ratio measures the percentage of assets supported by equity. The more the company is leveraged, the higher financial risk is.

$$Financial\ Leverage\ Ratio = \frac{Average\ total\ assets}{Average\ total\ equity} = \frac{1{,}327{,}600}{703{,}628} = 1.89$$

From the calculations above can be concluded that each dollar of equity supports 1.89 dollars of assets.

Interest Coverage Ratio

This ratio measures how many times a company can pay its interest expenses from its operating profit. A higher ratio indicates stronger solvency and makes it easier for the company to take on additional debt and with lower cost.

$$Interest\ Coverage\ Ratio = \frac{EBIT}{Interest\ Payments} = \frac{189{,}445}{12{,}480} = 15.18$$

From this example can be seen that this company can pay 15.18 times its interest expense. This number would put the company in a strong position to borrow debt. Note that in many cases, instead of EBIT, in this calculation is used EBITDA (earnings before interest, taxes, depreciation and amortization).

Profitability Ratios

Profitability ratios measure company's ability to generate returns compared to its expenses during a period of time. Profitability analysis can give a comprehensive view of the company's performance. Most common ratios used in profitability analysis include:

- **Gross Profit Margin**

- **Operating Profit Margin**

- **Pretax Margin**

- **Net Profit Margin**

- **Return on Assets – ROA**

- **Return on Equity – ROE**

- **Return on Total Capital**

Gross Profit Margin, Operating Profit Margin, Pretax Margin, and Net Profit Margin

These four ratios measure company's return on sales.

Gross Profit Margin

This ratio shows the percentage of revenue to cover all other expenses left after the cost of goods sold is covered. A high gross profit margin indicates the company is able to command a high price on its products relative to its production cost.

$$Gross\ Profit\ Margin = \frac{Gross\ profit}{Revenues} = \frac{392{,}431}{871{,}105} = 0.45$$

Operating Profit Margin

This ratio is a good indicator of the company's efficiency. A low operating profit margin (with a relative high gross profit margin) indicates that the company needs to better manage its operating costs.

$$Operating\ Profit\ Margin = \frac{Operating\ profit}{Rvenues} = \frac{188,445}{871,105} = 0.22$$

Pretax Margin

This ratio is a good indicator of a company's performance as it gives a more clear result on the overall operating performance of a company without the impact of taxes, as taxes are not a result of operations.

$$Pretax\ Margin = \frac{Income\ before\ tax\ (but\ after\ interest)}{Revenues} = \frac{176,964}{871,105} = 0.20$$

Net Profit Margin

This ratio shows the percentage of revenues left for the business after all the expenses have been deducted. A relative high number of net profit margin makes a company attractive to investors.

$$Net\ Profit\ Margin = \frac{Net\ Income}{Revenues} = \frac{133{,}633}{871{,}105} = 0.15$$

Return on Assets - ROA

This ratio measures what percentage of the investment in assets is returned back to the company each period in the form of net income. This indicator shows how efficient is management in using company's assets to generate returns.

$$Return\ on\ Assets = \frac{Net\ income}{Total\ assets} = \frac{133,633}{1,393,980} = 0,096 = 9.6\%$$

As can be seen, each period, this company returns 9.6% of its investment in assets through net income.

Return on Equity

This ratio measures what percentage of equity is returned in the form of profits, or how much net income is generated by every dollar of shareholders invested in the company.

$$Return\ on\ Equity = \frac{Net\ income}{Equity - preferred\ shares} =$$

$$\frac{133,633}{1,393,980} = 0,197 = 10.7\%$$

From this result can be concluded that every dollar of equity earns 10.7% return, or about 0.11 dollars.

Horizontal Analysis

Horizontal analysis, also know as trend analysis, is a financial analysis technique that shows trends in the data and changes in specific financial ratios over time. It is very important technique as it reveals important information on historical performance and helps managers understand and keep control of the important business variables. This technique is widely applicable in every business, especially to the ones, which have been in business for more than two years. It enables managers to spot on seasonality of the business and is very helpful tool in forecasting and planning.

Although it may not be applicable during the first couple years of the business, horizontal analysis can help entrepreneurs better understand the nature of their business. For instance, horizontal analysis can be used to show revenue over time and identify peaks over a year, which can later be used by managers to better prepare for busy seasons in terms of production, staff planning, and marketing spending. Besides, it helps entrepreneurs to better manage their cash using future cash flows. Based on the historical analysis of cash flow, you can determine the periods in which the company is in cash crisis. In fact, until the business breaks even it is highly preferred to do monthly projections of cash flow, balance sheet, and income statement. Doing a horizontal analysis you can see key business matrices over time and understand when the business need help.

In following figures, Figure 9 and 10, are presented one-year balance sheet and income statement, respectively, of a typical start-up. In this case, horizontal analysis of balance sheet help managers closely track level of cash, which is a very problematic asset for young entrepreneurs and helps them identify specific periods when the business may be facing cash crisis. On the other figure, figure 10, is presented income statement of the same business, which shows the level of income and expenses during the development stages of the business. In this case, we see the period when the business breaks even and actually nets a positive profit. Such analysis and projections are, of course, applied in mature businesses, as they need to follow key business measures over a period of time and identify trends.

Horizontal analysis technique is also used in presenting key ratios that we covered earlier. All, activity ratios, liquidity ratios, solvency ratios, and profitability ratios, are presented horizontally as well. For instance, performing trend analysis of liquidity ratios enables you to see if the business is improving its liquidity over time or is getting in liquidity troubles, which is very important information for managers and other decision-makers within the company. Another advantage of applying horizontal analysis is that they are easily projected in graphs, hence, more visible and easier to read. Figure 11 show three-year analysis of Net Revenue and Gross Profit for our XYZ company, which is easier to read, understand, and present.

Figure 9

	Jan	Feb	Mar	Apr	May	June	July	Aug	Sept	Oct	Nov	Dec	Total
Assets													
CurrentAssets													
Cash	$1,969.49	$10,178.66	$787.83	$732.00	$371.17	$210.34	$249.51	$488.68	$592.85	$597.02	$301.19	$10,105.36	$10,105.36
TotalCurrentAssets	$1,969.49	$10,178.66	$787.83	$732.00	$371.17	$210.34	$249.51	$488.68	$592.85	$597.02	$301.19	$10,105.36	$10,105.36
FixedAssets													
OfficeEquipment	$—	$—	$—	$—	$—	$—	$—	$—	$—	$—	$—	$—	$—
Depreciation	$—	$—	$—	$—	$—	$—	$—	$—	$—	$—	$—	$—	$—
TotalFixedAssets	$—	$—	$—	$—	$—	$—	$—	$—	$—	$—	$—	$—	$—
TotalAssets	$1,969.49	$10,178.66	$787.83	$732.00	$371.17	$210.34	$249.51	$488.68	$592.85	$597.02	$301.19	$10,105.36	$10,105.36
LiabilitiesandStockholder'sEquity													
CurrentLiabilities	$—	$—	$—	$—	$—	$—	$—	$—	$—	$—	$—	$—	$—
TotalCurrentLiabilities	$—	$—	$—	$—	$—	$—	$—	$—	$—	$—	$—	$—	$—
Long-termLiabilities	$—	$—	$—	$—	$—	$—	$—	$—	$—	$—	$—	$—	$—
TotalLong-termLiabilities	$—	$—	$—	$—	$—	$—	$—	$—	$—	$—	$—	$—	$—
TotalLiabilities	$—	$—	$—	$—	$—	$—	$—	$—	$—	$—	$—	$—	$—
OwnerEquity													
ContributedCapital	$10,000.00	$10,000.00	$10,000.00	$10,000.00	$10,000.00	$10,000.00	$10,000.00	$10,000.00	$10,000.00	$10,000.00	$10,000.00	$10,000.00	$10,000.00
RetainedEarning	$(8,030.51)	$9,821.34	$1,212.17	$(2,268.00)	$(5,628.83)	$(2,789.66)	$(2,750.49)	$(2,511.32)	$(2,402.98)	$(1,402.98)	$(10,698.81)	$(9,894.64)	$(9,894.64)
TotalStockholder'sEquity	$1,969.49	$10,178.66	$787.83	$732.00	$371.17	$210.34	$249.51	$488.68	$592.85	$597.02	$301.19	$10,105.36	$10,105.36
TotalLiabilitiesandStockholder'sEquity	$1,969.49	$10,178.66	$787.83	$732.00	$371.17	$210.34	$249.51	$488.68	$592.85	$597.02	$301.19	$10,105.36	$10,105.36

Figure 10

	Jan	Feb	Mar	Apr	May	June	July	Aug	Sept	Oct	Nov	Dec	Total
REVENUE													
Number of Acquisitions	3	4	4	5	2	2	2	2	1	1	1	1	28
Number of Sales	18	22	26	31	33	35	37	39	40	41	42	43	407
Revenue from Service	$8,800.00	$9,200.00	$11,600.00	$14,100.00	$15,300.00	$16,500.00	$17,700.00	$18,900.00	$19,000.00	$20,100.00	$21,200.00	$22,300.00	$190,700.00
Total Revenue	$8,800.00	$9,200.00	$11,600.00	$14,100.00	$15,300.00	$16,500.00	$17,700.00	$18,900.00	$19,000.00	$20,100.00	$21,200.00	$22,300.00	$190,700.00
Cost of Service	$450.83	$490.83	$490.83	$490.83	$490.83	$490.83	$490.83	$490.83	$490.83	$490.83	$490.83	$490.83	$5,289.96
Total Cost of Services	$450.83	$490.83	$490.83	$490.83	$490.83	$490.83	$490.83	$490.83	$490.83	$490.83	$490.83	$490.83	$5,289.96
Cost of Sales													
Sales Expenses	$440.00	$520.00	$520.00	$600.00	$560.00	$560.00	$560.00	$560.00	$560.00	$560.00	$560.00	$560.00	$7,240.00
Total Cost of Sales	$440.00	$520.00	$520.00	$600.00	$560.00	$560.00	$560.00	$560.00	$560.00	$560.00	$560.00	$560.00	$7,240.00
Gross Profit	$7,969.17	$8,189.17	$10,589.17	$13,009.17	$14,449.17	$15,649.17	$16,849.17	$18,049.17	$19,229.17	$20,329.17	$21,429.17	$22,529.17	$180,170.04
General and Administrative Expenses													
Acquisition Costs	$55.00	$40.00	$40.00	$25.00	$70.00	$70.00	$70.00	$70.00	$35.00	$35.00	$35.00	$35.00	$3,380.00
Application Development	$0.00	$0.00	$0.00	$0.00	$0.00	$0.00	$0.00	$0.00	$0.00	$0.00	$0.00	$0.00	$0.00
Advertising	$100.00	$100.00	$100.00	$100.00	$100.00	$100.00	$100.00	$100.00	$100.00	$100.00	$100.00	$100.00	$9,400.00
Other Marketing Expenses	$100.00	$100.00	$100.00	$100.00	$100.00	$100.00	$100.00	$100.00	$100.00	$100.00	$100.00	$100.00	$6,800.00
Owner's Salaries	$400.00	$400.00	$400.00	$400.00	$400.00	$400.00	$400.00	$400.00	$400.00	$400.00	$400.00	$400.00	$8,800.00
Payroll Taxes	$440.00	$440.00	$440.00	$440.00	$440.00	$440.00	$440.00	$440.00	$440.00	$440.00	$440.00	$440.00	$3,000.00
Rent	$50.00	$50.00	$50.00	$50.00	$50.00	$50.00	$50.00	$50.00	$50.00	$50.00	$50.00	$50.00	$1,200.00
Phone	$0.00	$100.00	$100.00	$100.00	$100.00	$100.00	$100.00	$100.00	$100.00	$100.00	$100.00	$100.00	$0.00
Depreciation	$0.00	$0.00	$0.00	$0.00	$0.00	$0.00	$0.00	$0.00	$0.00	$0.00	$0.00	$0.00	$0.00
Office Supplies	$0.00	$0.00	$0.00	$0.00	$0.00	$0.00	$0.00	$0.00	$0.00	$0.00	$0.00	$0.00	$100.00
Utilities													
Total General and Administrative Expenses	$1,895.00	$1,980.00	$1,980.00	$1,065.00	$1,810.00	$1,810.00	$1,810.00	$1,810.00	$1,775.00	$1,775.00	$1,775.00	$1,725.00	$64,060.00
TOTAL OPERATING EXPENSES	$1,895.00	$1,980.00	$1,980.00	$1,065.00	$1,810.00	$1,810.00	$1,810.00	$1,810.00	$1,775.00	$1,775.00	$1,725.00	$1,725.00	$64,060.00
Operating Income (EBIT)	$7,025.83	$7,790.83	$8,390.83	$11,055.83	$12,160.83	$13,160.83	$14,139.17	$15,139.17	$16,504.17	$17,504.17	$18,504.17	$19,504.17	$84,889.96
Interest													
Taxes													
NET INCOME	$7,025.83	$7,790.83	$8,390.83	$11,055.83	$12,160.83	$13,160.83	$14,139.17	$15,139.17	$16,504.17	$17,504.17	$18,504.17	$19,504.17	$84,889.96

Figure 11

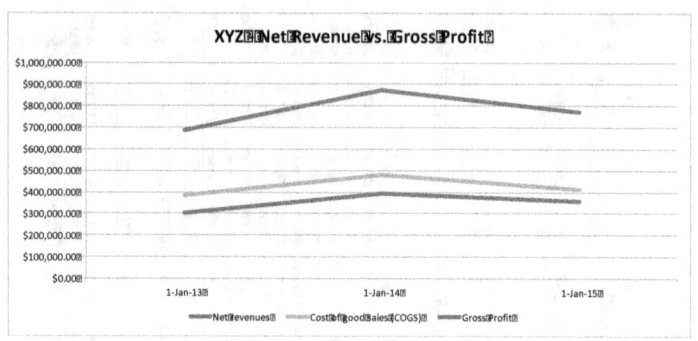

Further, horizontal analysis technique is highly applied in planning and budgeting. Horizontal analysis enables you to compare data over two or more periods of time; hence, provide a basis for understanding to where the company is headed. For instance, when budgeting net sales for the next fiscal year, you need to see how your net sales have been performing in month-to-month or year-to-year basis; hence, understand your growth rate and be able to project over that same rate.

Break-even Analysis

A break-even analysis for entrepreneurs and investors is extremely important to understand when the company will break even and start to generate profit. Break-even means that the business has reached the point when profits equal total costs. Of course, the sooner a business breaks even, the more sustainable it becomes and less headache to managers and investors.

To perform a break-even analysis, we should classify our costs into fixed costs and variable costs. Fixed costs are costs that are constantly incurred whatever the quantity of the products or services produced. Fixed costs include rent, manager's salary, utilities, taxes, interest expenses, and many others depending in the nature of the business. Those costs are extremely important to understand as they will not be direct participant in the production of the output, but they all have to be paid by the business. On the other hand, we have variable expenses, which include all the expenses that are incurred only when an additional product is produced.

Referring to the break-even formula:

Profit = Total Costs = Fixed Costs + Variable Costs

We understand that a business needs to generate enough profit to level total costs and break even.

To illustrate break-even analysis, we will use the following case:

XYZ produces pens, which cost $1 to produce and sell for $2. The pen is made of three raw materials A, B, C, which cost $0.5, $0.3, and $0.2, respectively. Additionally, the company has to pay rent of $1,000 per month, fixed salaries of $3,000, and utilities of $1,500 per month. So, XYZ's fixed costs are $5,500, and it costs it an additional $1 to produce a pen. How many units does XYZ need to sell to break even?

First, we identify fixed costs, which in our case are $5,500 per month. Second, we calculate gross profit per pen, which is: Selling price – Production costs = $2 - $1 = $1. Hence, for every pen XYZ sells it generates $1 in profit. Now we are ready to calculate break-even, as we know the variable cost and fixed costs, and now we divide fixed costs over gross profit:

Break-even = Fixed Costs/Gross Profit = $5,500/$1= 5,500 units.

Therefore, XYZ needs to sell 5,500 pens in order to break even.

Sensitivity Analysis

It is highly recommended for business managers to test the sensitivity of their business against different scenarios to build a more through business model and be prepared for different issues it may be facing in the future. Startup companies embody a high level of risk as they are new to the market and they do not have any history in the market. Hence, we have to be performing what-if analysis meaning what would happen with the business if everything goes as planned, what is the best-case scenario, and what is the worst-case scenario. Each of the scenarios should be done independent studies and presentations, and prepare three key financial statements we covered at the beginning.

Performing worst-case sensitivity analysis enables you to understand what happens to the business if things do not go as planned; in fact, they go against you. A critical point here would be analyzing your cash flow and cash amount you have. Would the company have enough money to resist trouble times and for how long it can last? Answering such question enables you better prepare for the challenges of your business.

Also, you should perform best-case analysis when the business turns out to be performing way better than expected, which is of course great news. However, you need to be prepared for such scenario and potentially have a good expansion plan in place.

Chapter 5

Manage your growth

You want to grow your company, right? There is an adage: "If you are not growing, you are dying."

This is a pretty easy concept to grasp. Think of your garden. What happens when you do not "tend" it? The weeds grow faster than the vegetables. If you don't water it, the whole thing dies.

Likewise, if you do not paint your house routinely, it begins peeling and deteriorating into an unsightly mess.

The same is true with your business. If not given the attention it deserves; it starts a downward spiral. Perishable items of inventory do exactly that – perish. Customers quit coming when the service they receive begins to deteriorate.

Critical steps for growth

The following steps are essential to managed growth. They are in no particular order because they are equal in importance to the success of your business growth.

Check everything

Check your account balances routinely. In most cases, it is not necessary to balance the checking accounts every day. On the other hand, you should check balances often enough to know where your company stands financially.

All spending decisions must be informed decisions. As I related earlier, I relied heavily on my homemade Excel spreadsheet to keep track of my cash flow position. Even then, I was caught off guard when Walt informed me that we were $30,000 overdrawn at the bank.

There is always the argument against micro-management. Employees need room for independence and personal creativity, and they need the right to fail.

I would like to rebut that argument by pointing out that it is your company. You are the one who is ultimately responsible for its success or failure. If you allow your business to go belly-up, the employees will just find another job. You, on the other hand, are tied to the success or failure of the business. If in fact, you lose your company, you must get up and try again.

Never let a one-time mistake of not checking everything rob you of your future. Recognize that it is only a stumbling block waiting to be turned into a stepping stone to your next success.

Believe me, I know from experience: It is easier to check everything and nip any problem in the bud than it is to start all over again.

Ask questions

Talk to everyone and ask questions. Ask your employees for ways to improve the operation of your business. Ask your customers what they would like to see happen in your business. Is there a product or service they would like to purchase from you? Are they happy with the quality of service you offer? Is there anything they wish that you or your employees would offer in the way of customer service?

Speaking of customer service, it should not be an oxymoron in your business. In our fast-paced world of 30-second sound bites, fast food, instant gratification at every level of our lives, it does not take a lot to stand out. A little TLC provided as part of the contact experience with your business will go a long way toward making your company stand out in the crowd.

I understand that I am a hard customer to please. But I can also tell you my predictions of a business heading to failure because of the way I was treated as a customer have been right many times.

Think back about your experiences. How many times have you received shoddy treatment, purchased an overpriced product or been refused a refund for an inferior purchase only to witness the closing of the business a few months later?

Sometimes we accept too much of the blame, saying as I just did, "I am a hard customer to please." Trust me, if they don't please you, they don't please others either.

When you ask your customers what you can do to improve their experience with your business, LISTEN to them!

Plan

Growth does not just happen. You may be one of the lucky ones who stumbles upon a formula that takes the world by storm. When that happens, count your lucky stars and hold on for dear life while you try to manage surging growth.

However, if you are more like the rest of the world, dependent on making your business successful one exhausting day at a time, plan your growth.

Were there products and services your customers inquired about when you talked with them? If so, examine the potential for additional profit by adding said product or service.

Do your due diligence, though. Just because one or even several customers talked about an item, it does not mean you can stock and sell it successfully. What quantities do you have to purchase to have a sufficient profit margin? Are there competitors better qualified to provide the item? Are they already selling it at a lower price than would allow a margin of profit for you?

Can you increase sales with your current location only or do you need to plan for additional locations? Can you control more of your local market by offering additional "more convenient" locations?

Your planning process needs all the due diligence and forethought of starting a new business. It is easier than your initial startup because of your experience in your marketplace. However, it cannot be assumed that opening a new location will automatically be a raging success.

Review

I suggest taking an afternoon (or morning) to review your monthly financial statement. In my book, "**Grow Your Business to Extreme Wealth**," I spent a considerable amount of time discussing due diligence for the purchase of an existing business. These techniques are an excellent way to review your business. Look at every line on your financial statement with a discriminating buyer's perspective. Would you buy your business? What improvements would you make? Are there product lines you should drop because of slow sales? Can those product lines be promoted efficiently for greater profitability? Are you understaffed or overstaffed? Is it possible to get increased productivity from your staff? Are you losing good people to your competitors? If so, is it a matter of pay levels or a sour corporate culture?

When your review is complete, make a plan of action. Check for unintended consequences. Be sure that fixing one area does not have an adverse impact in other areas of your business model.

Test your ideas

This is part of my "look before you leap" philosophy. I wish I could say all my thoughts are good ideas. Some are so good I have to ascribe them to divine influence.

Others are so bad it is easy to see they came from indigestion. The challenge is that it is sometimes hard to tell them apart.

That is why testing is so important. When you devise your test, make sure the sample is large enough for conclusive results and small enough not to have a damaging impact on your business.

For example, do not reduce your commission structure to increase your profit margin and end up losing your best salespeople. Good people are too hard to recruit and train.

Watch out for a self-fulfilling prophecy. Design your test for a fair result. I like to joke that you can substantiate any position with a survey by the way you word the questions. If you control the results, there is no point in running the test. If you prefer to do it your way, go for it and hope for the best.

Attend seminars

What a great way to stay in touch with the changes in your industry. I like going for all the new ideas. A word of advice: If you are like most of us, burning the candle at both ends, be sure to get at least two good night's sleep before going to the seminar.

Not only is it embarrassing to fall asleep on the speaker, but you will also miss the great ideas the speaker will prompt as you listen to the presentation.

One thing I have learned is to glean information from the other attendees. Some of them are actually more knowledgeable than the speaker. In addition, they are working in the trenches the same way you are.

Chapter 6

Your attitude about money

There is an often-misquoted passage in the Bible referring to money. The New Testament book of I Timothy 6:10: "For the love of money is the root of all evil: which while some coveted after, they have erred from the faith, and pierced themselves through with many sorrows."

Many people misquote it to say "Money is the root of all evil." There is nothing wrong with money or the pursuit of success financially!

I think it is worth our consideration in the context of owning a business today. The political stance seems to be that businesses and business owners are evil and should be taxed higher so we can take care of the needs of the poor.

Taking care of the poor sounds good at first blush. However, when you dig a little deeper, some questions come up. If we tax the business owner out of business, who will then take care of the poor? Does the provision of a job in and of itself provide care for the poor?

As a person who grew up in poverty the son of alcoholic parents, I learned to work for food and clothing. I have a sense of pride in my accomplishment and ability to provide for my family. Do we rob people of their self-respect when we provide all their needs via a handout we finance by taxing the "rich"?

Yes, greed and corruption are wrong and should enter into our discussion. There were two sides to the government bailout of the financial industry. One was, why should the American taxpayer foot the bill for the failure of a greedy business owner? Two, would a total financial collapse of our economy have been a better alternative?

This is not a book about ethics, politics or corruption in business. Nor is it about the church or our elected officials.

There is another version of the Bible passage I quoted earlier. The same passage in the "Message Bible," a modern attempt to put the Bible in contemporary language, reads "But if it's only money these leaders are after, they'll self-destruct in no time. Lust for money brings trouble and nothing but trouble. Going down that path, some lose their footing in the faith completely and live to regret it bitterly ever after."

My point is simply this – be friends with your money. Don't have an affair with it. Lusting after money has the potential to destroy your business if allowed to take its natural course.

It is hard to make sound business decisions when your focus is on your profit and to heck with the customer, your employee, your stockholders or anyone else standing in the way of your MONEY!

Sound business decisions are possible only when the needs of your customer, employee and stockholder are balanced with the needs of the business to operate with a realistic margin of profit.

I pray for the success of your business. More people working creates more tax revenue. More people working leaves fewer "poor" people needing assistance.

Please do not attack me. I know I have not addressed minimum wage, international trade issues, unions or the myriad other financial concerns we all have.

This book is about how you can more successfully operate your business. Can we make it better by taking one positive step forward? YES! So let's do it.

Let's make your business more profitable. Then you can decide how much you want to donate to charity. You can vote your conscience for our political leaders, and together we can have a hand in addressing the issues we face in our country and around the world.

Do not farm it out to "trusted" employees

If you are like me, there is a temptation to hire it out. I dislike paperwork. That is one reason Walt was able to float the payroll at the bank. I was not watching closely.

Believe me, Walt was a reliable employee and personal friend. His actions were not meant to hurt me or the business. He was just in over his head.

Here is a challenge for you. Farm it out and then keep a close eye on it without micro-managing. Got it?

Nobody said operating your business successfully is easy. Let me throw one more dig in. The "greedy" business owner is not greedy; he/she is a hard-working person who overcame the obstacles to building a successful business. My hat is off to you!

Contracts –

"worst case scenario" covered.

As you recall, Harriet was my business partner's wife. She spent their money, which was committed to our business, on personal things like redecorating and refurnishing their home.

Because of her spending, we no longer had the committed money to fund our business start-up. Remember money is one of the most common reasons for business failure.

You see the impending failure coming as a result of money (or lack thereof). Now let me explain how the issue was exacerbated.

We still had an unfunded partnership. When drawing up the partnership agreement, it never dawned on me that Harriet would spend the money. As a result, there was no provision in the agreement for lack of performance.

To keep the business up and running, I now had to come up with the money to buy out my "useless" partner and the money he did not provide because of Harriet's uncontrolled spending.

Fortunately, I was able to accomplish the impossible. The start-up was successful, and I survived the storm.

Learn from my mistake. Expect the unexpected. Spend money on a competent contract attorney and stand your ground in the early stage negotiations.

Think about what can go wrong with a property lease opportunity. Think about the "what-ifs" when negotiating with a potential partner. Think about how an employee may react to a new policy.

Chapter 7

Working on your Business

Brian owned a successful digital marketing company. He enjoyed working on projects for his clients but disliked the business side.

Putting together proposals with the pressure of finding that fine line between charging enough to make a profit and losing the prospective customer to a lower quote just did not fit Brian's personality.

Once he got the project approval, he needed to hire the subcontractors to perform the work. The alternative scared Brian because it meant establishing a higher fixed overhead with a weekly payroll to meet, whether he had work or not. That added to the pressure.

Fortunately for Brian, one of his clients recognized the value of his talent and offered him a full-time job doing what he enjoyed doing the most – working on projects.

For the risk-taker – all true entrepreneurs are risk-takers at heart – there would have been no problem. We have a great product. There is a proven need in the marketplace. We can hire competent people to work and make a profit on their effort. Here is what we are going to do. Set up a marketing campaign to bring in more leads than we realistically service. That will give us the ability to bid a higher price because we are not desperate for a close on each prospect.

Which are you? Do you prefer to do the work of your company or would you rather build your company? Either is fine; you just need to focus on one or the other.

A financial analysis of your business will help you set a strategy for growth. Your decisions will be based on facts. Be sure to get comparative results from other businesses of your approximate size and in your industry. A favorite saying of mine is, "There is always room at the top for one more."

Working on your business is more important than working in your business. I attended a seminar on business growth quite a number of years ago in Southern California.

During one of the breakout sessions, I learned the importance of working on, not just working in your business.

Ben purchased a McDonald's franchise that just didn't hum like he thought it should. It was losing money. Ben related how he fired a cashier to save money and worked behind the counter himself to take care of the customers.

One especially busy day, Ben started thinking about how hard he was working for the pittance of money he had paid the high school girl to run the cash register.

Then and there he decided to hire a new cashier. He went home and sat by the pool with a cold drink and began to assess his business and, more importantly, his life. Had he spent all that money on a

McDonald's franchise so he could earn the wages of a part-time cashier?

After about a week of contemplation, Ben decided to purchase a second McDonald's. This time, he found a better location and enjoyed enough success to buy a third and then fourth franchise.

Ben found great success by working on his business instead of in his business. Oh yes, I almost forgot to tell you, the first store he purchased never did make any money for him. It was a wrong location barely able to pay the overhead instead of the standard profit stream of a McDonald's franchise.

If you are content to work in your business, you probably could have earned the same amount of money working for someone else and with a whole lot less stress. It is possible you may decide it is right for you.

If so, sell it. Take the profit and buy something you are better suited to work on, not in!

Understanding growth levels

An article in the Harvard Business Review divided businesses into five stages:

Existence

This stage can be loosely described as turning the idea or thought into an existing start-up. The owners have provided the capital through savings, debt, family or other partners to launch the business. Some label this stage survival, because it is the most difficult to survive.

The management style typically is the owner doing everything, especially sales and marketing. He/she is micromanaging every facet of the business, even the processes that are outsourced.

One of the businesses I started, Diamond Rose Shears, LLC, focuses on the beauty industry. I invented a scissors sharpening machine and system that restores haircutting scissors to their factory cutting condition.

As the inventor, I was involved in every detail, including the manufacturing of the machine. I developed the system with procedures for the sharpening process.

First, we (my wife, Coleen, and I) chose the brand name Musashi Shears for our proprietary haircutting scissors line. Then six or eight manufacturing companies were tested to find the best quality. We wanted quality and pricing that would allow an affordable pricing level for the end user – professional barbers and hair stylists.

Like many startups, money was an issue. Rather than hiring it out, the task of designing marketing material, developing videos and other jobs necessary for starting a new business fell on my shoulders.

I share this to explain why many startups fail in the existence stage. Most of us do not have the necessary skills to do all of the jobs required to start a successful business.

Like other successful owners, I persevered. I worked long and hard, got lucky and developed a successful business.

When planning a new business, expanding an existing business or growing by acquisition, it is vital you count the costs. Do you have the necessary skills for the task anticipated? Are you able to commit the time? Are there people available at your current stage of growth to assume your duties, freeing your time for the next stage of growth? Or are the funds available to hire the talent you need?

Survival

Yes, wipe the sweat off your brow – both the emotional sweat of worry and the physical sweat of hard work.

If you have made it through the survival stage, congratulations! You have demonstrated the viability of your concept. You have proven that customers will spend money on your product or service. The business has developed cash flow at a level to pay expenses and provide for your personal living expenses.

Don't forget, even at the survival level, you must set aside the money for unexpected items, such as equipment replacement, and as a buffer for an unexpected downturn in your industry, both locally and nationally.

Imagine that you started a home construction business a year or two before the most recent housing crash. I personally recall the struggle to survive the 21% interest rates under the Carter Administration. Wait, I did not survive with my real estate business. I closed it and moved on to develop a business brokerage and merger and acquisition consulting firm.

There are times when it is best to abandon the sinking ship before it takes you to the bottom of the sea. I know the captain is supposed to go down with the boat, but that is lousy advice for an entrepreneur. If something drastic happens in your business, the better part of valor is to face the facts and do what is necessary to survive individually. If the extreme event was because of your failure, learn from it and move on.

As I am writing this section, the news is reporting that billionaire Richard Branson has survived a bicycle crash. He said two things: "I literally saw my life flashing before my eyes" as a bump in the road sent him catapulting into the pavement in front of him. Then he said, "My attitude has always been, if you fall flat on your face, at least you're moving forward."

I agree wholeheartedly. You will never get anywhere without moving. Take the actions necessary to get through the survival stage and move forward to the next level of your business growth!

Lawrence L. Steinmetz, author of

"How to Sell at Margins Higher Than Your Competitors: Winning Every Sale at Full Price, Rate, or Fee," says that to survive, a small business must move through four stages of growth.

1. Direct supervision To leave this stage, the owner has to learn to be a manager and how to delegate to others.

2. Supervised supervision Hiring or promoting people to management is critical to growth. Be sure not to move too quickly. This is especially hard for individuals who have worked for a larger company and have grown accustomed to the management

hierarchy. Moving from a mid- or upper-level management position to the owner of a start-up company can be dangerous. Hiring people before the sales volume will support them can sink the ship and drive your growth back instead of forward.

3. Indirect control Now the owner has to move up another notch, giving the senior managers more control. This may mean the middle management level gets a little messy and margins suffer a little as the organization begins to build quality in the whole management team. All you

perfectionists need to understand that it is not always going to get done with your level of efficiency.

4. Divisional management At this stage, the company has arrived. It now has the personnel and resources to move forward on its own.

Success

Your business is humming along successfully, with cash accumulating in the bank for operations and profit. Your staff is functioning well enough so that when you take a vacation, your business does not come to a screeching halt.

Now, what do you do? Many companies never go beyond this stage of growth. They are unwilling to use their success to push to the next level. Moving forward from our comfort zone is always risky.

The effort of getting to this point may have taken a psychological or even a physical toll on your health.

On the other hand, you may want to jump forward to the new challenge. In my book, "Grow your Business to Extreme Wealth," I discuss using a strong business as a base for a roll-up, a franchise model or even a base for national expansion. What do you want to do with yours? At 72, I am still watching for opportunities. But then, if I could do anything I wanted to do, I would do what I am doing now. I like business ownership. The challenge of growth is more fun than golf, and believe me; I like golf.

Some business owners at this stage decide to pursue hobbies, nonprofit organizations or even running for political office. A successful business can make any of these activities possible.

Take-off

In this exciting stage of your growth, the key factors will be how to grow rapidly and how to finance that growth. The management requirements are much the same as discussed earlier in the indirect control stage described by Lawrence Steinmetz.

As the owner, can you delegate responsibilities to others and improve managerial effectiveness? If not, your take-off growth phase is going to go up in the smoke of management frustration, to say nothing of your frustration.

Maturity

Your company now has a life of its own. It is similar to watching a child finish college and get his first real job. Even with a new home, marriage and a family, your child is still your child, but things are different. Your baby is all grown up and making a life for himself.

In this case, it is your business baby that has grown up and left home for good.

www.ingramcontent.com/pod-product-compliance
Lightning Source LLC
Chambersburg PA
CBHW071428180526
45170CB00001B/266